The Spirit of
Community

The Spirit of Community

The Power of the Sacraments in The Christian Community

Ulrich Meier

Floris Books

Translated by Matthew Barton

First published as *Einigkeit der Einzelnen: Sakrament und Gemeinschaftsbildung* by Verlag Urachhaus in 2022
First published in English by Floris Books, Edinburgh in 2024
© 2022 Verlag Urachhaus
English version © 2024 Floris Books

 Also available as an eBook

British Library CIP available
ISBN 978-178250-896-0

Contents

Note: The English ritual translations differ slightly between the different continents. The British version is quoted here, but there may be minor discrepancies between translations in North America, Southern Africa or Australia and New Zealand.

Foreword

Christianity was born in the hearts and minds of the followers of Jesus: Jewish men and women whose prayers and rituals were founded on the experience of a God who was deeply involved in human history, a God who was at work in the world, creating and sustaining it, and guiding the affairs of human beings.

As Christianity spread beyond its Jewish origins, it became important to find new ways of speaking and thinking about the disciples' experience of Jesus Christ, which had transformed the lives of the first Christians. The culture of Hellenism, with its rich heritage of Greek philosophy, poetry and drama, became the medium for communicating the message. The dominant philosophical strand of this Greek cultural heritage at the time of Christ located the real in an unchanging realm of being far beyond ordinary earthly experience. It was a view of the world that the logical thinking of the Latin mind took to an extreme. But if the most real things are to be found in the realm of pure being, then our picture of the world ultimately becomes static, and this contrasted strongly with the Hebrew experience of a God who was active in history.

There was, however, another strand of Greek thinking that persisted down through the centuries and which received a new infusion of life in the twentieth century through the work of the modern philosopher Alfred North Whitehead (1861–1947). This became known as process philosophy, along with its sister movement, process theology. This way of thinking about the world sees what is real not in unchanging, eternal states, but in processes: in growth and becoming. It allows us to see the divine at work in the world through evolution and change.

In an individual's life, it is this process of growth and becoming with its various milestones that the sacraments of The Christian Community celebrate. They are an opportunity for people to reflect on their lives, to take their bearings on their own spiritual journeys, and find a renewed energy and enthusiasm for the path ahead. But these moments are not just important for those receiving the sacraments; they are of significance to the wider community that also participates in them and supports its individual members. The names given to The Christian Community at its birth bear this out. It is not a 'new church', rather it strives to be a community – a place where we work for a common purpose – and a movement for renewal. Of course, after one hundred years, we are no longer as new as we once were in 1922. Our question now must be whether we are still faithful to the revolutionary idea of a church that sees itself as a path, not a goal; that issues an invitation, not instructions; that seeks to release the potential of each human being as they find their activity, their community, their task in the world.

In this introduction to the sacraments of The Christian Community, Ulrich Meier makes an important contribution to this revolution in our thinking. There is much here that is unconventional. How many books on the seven sacraments in The Christian Community have been written that tread the familiar path from baptism to last anointing! This book begins with the last anointing and the rituals surrounding death, which allows us to see death itself as a moment in a greater process. This then opens the door for a contemplation of the other sacraments, not as events that confer upon us a state of grace, but as focal points where divine and human initiative flow together, and from there become active in the wider world.

Tom Ravetz

Introduction

A person becomes a Christian not through family tradition or membership of a church, but through personal experience and conviction. Sacramental life in Christian congregations is nowadays founded on the free participation of their members, motivated by their inner resolve and the quest for life's transformation. The present volume seeks to show how the seven Christian sacraments can form the basis and provide inspiration for building a diverse community.

Declining traditions and a new openness

The importance of Christian tradition and ecclesiastical life has markedly declined over the past fifty years, along with basic knowledge of the Bible and Christian festivals. Although we might regard this as a regrettable loss of Christian culture, the decline in traditional religious observance has also meant the disappearance of all kinds of misunderstandings and aberrations that developed over the long history of Christianity.

Educators of a former era often cited an all-seeing divine power to strengthen their own weak authority and compel 'moral conduct' in their charges, but few would resort to such a view of God today. Yet at the same time, in my experience, children and adolescents relate to Christian stories and religious experiences with an astonishing degree of openness, being less hampered by pre-existing modes of thought and speech that might otherwise erect a barrier to them. And parents no longer feel the need to pass on their own rejection of religion either – they are more open-minded towards questions of faith and see them as a self-evident topic of discussion.

While the radical atheism that has emerged in public discourse, especially since the events of September 11, 2001, sees every kind of religious conviction as the root of terrorism and warmongering, on the other hand there are authors with a surprisingly open and unprejudiced view of religion. I would like to cite two examples.

The philosopher Jean-Luc Nancy, having honed his thinking through engagement with modern philosophy, rediscovered religion and Christianity anew. A former atheist, he was converted to 'absence-theism'[1] and from then on celebrated the 'unfinished' nature of Christianity, which he discerns among other things in its 'absent' but nevertheless promised God. And in 2019, the journalist Evelyn Finger, chief editor of the 'Beliefs and Doubts' section of the weekly paper *Die Zeit*, wrote as follows in its Easter issue under the heading 'Cross and Church':

> What is this Cross in reality? Certainly not a threatening symbol but rather the sign of a defeat: God becomes human and amongst humankind he underwent the worst imaginable suffering … Only after this does the bright moment of resurrection come. Jesus' earthly defeat inexplicably transforms itself into something super-earthly. Into a hope. Into a promise of redemption. We can believe this or not. But what follows from it for the Church's relationship with the world? First of all this: that it stands, with its message, at the threshold between a profane and a sacred realm; that the Church is in the world, but is not of this world.

A new religious community culture

These few sentences already point to a new kind of discourse that seems vital to me for seeking religious renewal in the way The Christian Community does: any tone of paternalism or of knowing better than others will close off rather than open gateways. This does not mean that Christian teachings should be in some way diluted or relativised. What matters above all is the intention with which they are offered. In the second example above this becomes discernible in the simple statement, 'We can believe this or not.' This phrase should not be misunderstood as an expression of indifference or disinterest; rather it should be taken as an indication that we are indeed free to explore, or not, the contents of faith as we wish.

It also seems to me that any productive discussion between Christians relies upon them relinquishing all attempts to establish a 'valid' or ultimate explanation of Christian belief. We must be willing to live with perplexity and astonishment at things that are fundamentally inexplicable – such as the indwelling of God in a human being or the overcoming of death at the resurrection. In the twenty-first century it can no longer be a question of whether knowledge is superior to belief or vice versa. Instead we must understand how both belief *and* knowledge can work together to make spiritual insight and experience fruitful. This involves seeing error and doubt in a more positive light, and learning to value the unsolved questions with which we live.

In her book *Reading the Bible: The Power of the Sacred Texts*,[2] the Evangelical theologian Uta Pohl-Patalong offers various methods to help Christians in Bible groups engage with the contents of holy scripture. Representing her 'Bibliology' method, she writes in her introduction that in the new millennium, in all Christian churches, a greater interest is now apparent in the kinds of experiences that arise from immersing oneself in Biblical pictures and words, both in a group and on one's own. Here, too, the focus is not primarily on explanations, but on opening gateways in our engagement with the Bible.[2]

Over the past one hundred years, The Christian Community has sought to build community through the cultivation and preparation of the sacraments, with the priest serving as a guide and counsellor rather than issuing congregations with authoritarian edicts. The freedom of doctrine and belief rooted in this outlook can be seen as requiring mutual relinquishment of a patronising or domineering approach among Christians.

Sacrament as initiative

On Mount Sinai Moses received two revelations: the Ten Commandments and the form of worship for the Israelites. A promise is bound up with both: in the Sinai commandments an inner path of schooling is given through which every individual prepares themselves for the coming of the Messiah; and in the founding of the rites of worship, which looked forward to their fulfilment in the temple in Jerusalem, pride of place is given to a celebration of the presence of God who unites himself with his people.

In Christianity, participation in the act of worship was seen as the fulfilment of a Church commandment and, ultimately, as a condition for achieving a salvation that was not available outside of the institution. As a result of this narrow view, the celebration of the sacraments during worship seem to represent the passive fulfilment of a duty externally imposed. In stark contrast to this stands a very different view of sacramental participation, which sees that, with every act of worship, a space is created in which God can be present.

Community and the individual

Whenever an individual considers joining a community, the first question that usually preoccupies them is what will they gain from becoming a member and what will membership demand of them? They might wonder which of their desires will be fulfilled by participating in the group, and what, by contrast, they might have to surrender in order to belong to it. How will the expected friction between self and group impact their life? Is there likely to be a danger that they will have to suppress and adapt themselves to such a degree that they can no longer experience their essential nature? Or will they end up asserting themselves so strongly that conflict with other members of the group will soon develop? These issues ultimately lead to the question of whether the individual serves the community or the community serves the individual.

In Jesus' dispute with the Pharisees about picking heads

of grain on the Sabbath, the answer to this question is clearly apparent in relation to religious law: 'Then he said to them, "The Sabbath was made for man, not man for the Sabbath"' (Mark 2:27). This does not however imply that the fundamental tension between individual and community has been resolved.

On December 12, 1918, shortly after the end of the First World War, Rudolf Steiner gave a lecture on the life of society in which he spoke about both the social and antisocial impulses of the human soul and spirit. He saw these as an oscillation between two extremes, neither of which could fully develop without the other. The idea of 'social requirements', much discussed at the time, was justified on the grounds that the individual's need for self-assertion and self-isolation required balancing with social structures.[3] In the reality of social interplay, therefore, 'I' and 'we' should not be seen as fixed entities in conflict with one another, but as part of a process of breathing. The mature I then no longer sees itself in tension between adaptation and opposition, but seeks out periods of loneliness for itself in order to become free again for life in community. In 1937, Dietrich Bonhoeffer summed this up in his book *Life Together*: 'Whoever cannot be alone should beware community. Whoever is not part of a community, should beware being alone.'[4]

This points to the needs of both the individual and the community, conditions which, arising from a seemingly static opposition between 'I' and 'we', can lead to fruitful reciprocity. Here the I does not experience community either as a threat to its self-realisation or as a substitute for it. And the community so organises itself that, rather than seeing its parts and members as contradicting the good of the whole, it views them instead as the potential for its enrichment and fulfilment.

Awakening to oneself through the other

A further level of community development comes into view when we turn our attention to how it germinates in the encounter between one I and another. In the lecture referred to above, Rudolf Steiner speaks of the 'primary sociological phenomenon' that acts as impetus and counter-impetus between human beings: a subtle interplay between sleep and wakefulness. The tendency to fall asleep, he says, is an expression of social drives, whereas a 'continual resistance, continual rebellion' against this tendency is prompted by our antisocial drives. What follows from this? Between loss of self as we devote ourselves to the other and self-assertion as we act upon the other – by turns 'falling asleep' in a social sense and 'awakening' to our antisocial drives – the I is unsettled and the unity of our inner being is weakened. In human encounters the soul shows itself to be a system that, still preserving itself as it opens, can never entirely isolate itself as it closes off. In defining ourselves we experience ourselves as we have become, whereas in opening to all that is other than us, we learn of our potential for further development.

Every fruitful mode of learning is based on this soul-breathing between an unconscious absorption of otherness and the wakeful assertion of self. If we were to preserve only what is our own, our growth would come to a standstill, just as it would if we were to blindly incorporate everything alien to us. In alternating between the delicate sleep of surrender and the gentle awakening to ourselves, integration and appropriation occur. All learning and inner development is a dialogic process that depends on specific encounters. In other words, without community the individual cannot find themselves anew; without a 'you', the I cannot grow; without dialogue with another, our own being dwindles.

This description of human encounter and community-building can become a religious principle of growth founded on the strength of union. But it applies first and foremost to every encounter between the human being and God. In the New Testament there is the promise of Jesus Christ that 'where two or three gather in my name, there am I with them' (Matt. 18:20). In the interplay of human meetings sought in the name of Christ, a kind of vessel is created in which he can be present. Thus, human community and the presence of God are two elements that make possible the sacraments (whose literal meaning is 'means of healing').

For the third element, the space created through dialogue opens 'downwards', as it were, in order to take up earthly substance and lead it towards transubstantiation through the sacramental process.

The creative potential of Christian communities

To regard Christian sacramentalism only as a deed of God acting upon his 'human creature', or the earth only as a 'means to an end', would be a narrow view of things. 'Earth' in the religious sense also always implies 'creation' – inconceivable without its origins in the creator God, but requiring transformation to the same degree that the human being does. We are not only 'creatures' but also called upon to become creators ourselves. As such, we are not only receivers but co-creative participants in the deeds of God amongst humankind and upon the earth. Whoever gathers with others in community in the name of Christ at the same time opens up a religious dialogue in which they can become, not only a partner with their companions, but also a partner of God in the healing of humanity and the earth.

1.

Anointing: The Art of Dying

The celebration of death in the sacrament of the last anointing, which also includes the last blessing and burial rites, can open the hearts of participants to the all-embracing community that exists between the living and the dead.

In The Christian Community, the way we relate to suffering and dying, and engage with those who have died and the loved ones they've left behind, plays an important role in the life of our congregation. Our burial rites and services in memory of the dead also repeatedly lead people to an encounter with the world of death and the dead, enabling them to sensitise their souls to this key realm of Christian life.

Overcoming the sharp division between life and death makes possible what may be the keenest experience of community we can have as human beings. But how can this help the active shaping of communities?

Befriending death

In her book *The Human Condition*,[1] Hannah Arendt counts among the basic conditions of human life not only 'natality', that is the basic fact of being born, but also mortality. In becoming man, Christ takes on both of these attributes and incorporates them into his being. In so doing, and in his conquest of death, he lends dying a new meaning. The beginning of life out of divine creation now no longer has to lead to the God-sundered death brought about by the Fall, but, since Golgotha, we can experience in dying the beginning of a new kind of 'life in God' that is raised out of temporality.

It has become increasingly apparent today how impoverished a society becomes if it only sees death as the tragic end of a unique earthly biography. Such a society stands helplessly before questions of fate and human development, and suffers from a loss of meaning and spirituality. This suffering does not find any comfort in superficial platitudes or unfounded trust in some vague, transcendental existence that seems remote from actual reality.

However, if we relinquish the idea of there being an absolute division between the world of the living and that of the dead, then this enlarges our perspective of human community. When we gather with this in mind, we can consider that such a gathering goes beyond those who are physically present to include the soul-spiritual proximity of those who were and continue to be connected with individuals and the community. Many sacramental prayers speak directly of the common element uniting the living and the dead in Christ. In seeking a transformation of the world, we not only stand upon the shoulders of those who have gone before us, but, in the knowledge that we are pursuing with them a shared path towards Christ, we can gain inspiration and strength from them. At the same time, our accompaniment of the dead upon their further journey can find enlargement and fulfilment in the congregation. The Christian altar in its dual form of grave and table has long been seen as the place where the living and the dead meet and fortify each other in the Christ offering.

A willingness to accept death, whenever it may come, stands in lively tension with the will for life. But these two things are not mutually exclusive. Learning to hold the earthly and spiritual dimensions in balance through a proper art of living, can help us overcome feelings of restlessness and inner paralysis that lead our lives into too narrow a dimension. What aspects of community-building can spring from the fact that people develop a 'preparedness for dying' and meet together with this outlook? The befriending of death resonates as a fine and subtle tone within all community culture: a sense of the importance of things, a love of life that is nourished by the proximity of death, and a longing for forgiveness and reconciliation, as well as an acceptance of failure, weakness and illness.

Seeing death as an essential part of life does not rob death of its grandeur and uniqueness as the most powerful transformation of our existence. Rather, fully accepting our mortality can lead to an unexpected intensification of our sense of being alive. The essayist Matthias Claudius[2] called death a 'friend', and thus invested the 'art of dying', or *Ars moriendi*, with an intimate and, at the same time, life-enhancing aspect.[3]

Mourning and spiritual enrichment

What are the practical initiatives that Christian congregations can take if they wish to cultivate this kind of community-building? Initially this can take the form of active participation in mourning and memorials. In modern remembrances of the dead, a one-dimensional glorification of the departed has increasingly given way to a more living and life-affirming picture of them. We need no longer attend such ceremonies as passive witnesses and mere observers but can participate in them actively, finding our own way in and through grief that does not anxiously hold fast to more or less incomprehensible tenets. In discussion groups we can engage with the issues that death raises for us. Grief does not have to isolate people but, through a culture of support, can signify a strengthening of both the individual and the community.

Sharing our life with the dead does not need to involve only a cultivation of memories of them. We can experience how they work out of their world and into ours and are present in our lives, which gives rise to a truly consoling, religious mood towards dying, death and continuing life. And this corresponds to a sense of the presence of God that is not satisfied with the prospect of a 'Last Judgement' but gives serious credence to the words of Christ: 'I am with you always, to the very end of the age' (Matt. 28:20).

2.

Baptism: A Festival of Recognition

When adults look upon a child, they can contemplate their own spiritual origins in a world of the unborn. Children's devotion can awaken a religious sense of life in those who live with them that can help them reconnect with the meaning and strength of our source in the divine. In this sense, community can be experienced as a reuniting of 'God's children'.

New beginnings

Hermann Hesse's well-known line of poetry, 'And magic lives in every new beginning…'[1] points to a biographical reality that we can experience in the presence of every newborn child. Parents and friends experience the beginning of human life as a unique wonder. Beyond all biological facts, this wonder can be seen as a faint reflection of the human being's existence in the spiritual world before birth. In The Christian Community, the sacrament of baptism does not so much mark the soul's entry into community with the divine, for it is already united with God, as it does serve as a sign of the soul's willingness to continue to live 'out of its divine spirit goals' determined in the life before birth. The fact that, in baptism, we acknowledge and affirm the divine nature of the soul, may be one of the reasons why parents today still ask for this sacrament despite a general waning in ecclesiastical and religious traditions.

The South Korean philosopher Byung-Chul Han characterises the potential of rituals as follows: 'The symbol (Greek *symbolon*) originally signifies a sign of recognition between two guests ... Symbolic perception as recognition is one that discerns a lasting and enduring quality.'[2]

According to Han, rituals transform our 'being in the world' into a 'being at home'. He sees it as a matter of regret that our modern civilisation is losing this power of recognition through its communications technology, which presents fleeting aspects of the new as ever-changing novelty.

As Christians we can experience a wholesome redress of this one-sided tendency when, in rituals, we celebrate our human existence as a recognition of the divine, and thereby discover what our life before birth can signify for our further existence. Every encounter with the world, with other people and with ourselves, can unfold new layers of

meaning and importance through a sense of re-encounter.
The magic, joyful experience of accord surfaces when we
experience that this, too, is I: a new, more comprehensive
and yet, at the same time, a more familiar aspect of myself
that I recognise in such encounters.

The name

The Bible speaks of two beginnings that mark key religious
turning points: the creation of the world out of God, and the
re-enlivening impulse given to that creation through the death
and resurrection of Jesus Christ. Against this encompassing
background we also gain sight of a sanctification of all human
initiatives, every new beginning that connects with the
source and goal of all unfolding in God. We can gratefully
acknowledge our origin in the creative initiative of God for
the world – the strength for every kind of beginning connects
our own human beginning with his resurrection from death.

The Easter stories in the Gospels, with their encounters
between the disciples and the resurrected Christ, highlight an
initially frightening and disconcerting experience followed,
however, by the joyful and healing character of recognition.
On Easter morning, Mary Magdalene mistakes Christ for
the gardener and only recognises him when he speaks her
name (John 20:14–18). At Emmaus, it is not until the end
of the encounter, with the gesture of breaking bread, that

recognition comes to the disciples, although this had begun to stir subliminally as they journeyed together: 'Were not our hearts burning within us while he talked with us on the road…?' (Luke 24:32). On Easter evening the gathered disciples only recognise him again when he shows them his stigmata (John 20:19–22).

Birth and rebirth

What occurs in these experiences gives the promise of futurity both to their community with Christ and to themselves, one that could not have been expected but which was nevertheless already prefigured and prophesied. In the night-time conversation between Jesus and Nicodemus, we find a pointer that can be recognised again 'in daylight':

> 'How can someone be born when they are old?'
> Nicodemus asked. 'Surely they cannot enter a
> second time into their mother's womb to be born!'
> Jesus answered, 'Very truly I tell you, no one can
> enter the kingdom of God unless they are born of
> water and the Spirit. Flesh gives birth to flesh, but
> the Spirit gives birth to spirit. You should not be
> surprised at my saying, "You must be born again."'
> (John 3:4–7)

The tension between bodily/physical birth on the one hand, and rebirth 'from above', was something that the early Christians related to the inner turning point of their baptism. They saw their religious longing for a second birth out of the spirit, leading not to death but to eternal life, as being fulfilled through baptism founded in the power of the resurrected one. In this light, every Christian deed becomes the spirit-filled beginning of new life, a sacramental act of baptism extending far beyond the church celebration of a child's christening.

'Become as children'

What does this Christian self-conception have to do with community-building? What aspect of childlikeness comes into play here? As people who have been baptised and who baptise in turn, we experience community through our origins in, and connection with, God. We perceive each other in the shared quality of recognition. In this sense Christian religiosity is rooted not only in the cultivation of remembrance of events at the time of Christ, when Christ was 'bodily' present among human beings, but in a community-creating memory of human beings' pre-birth connection with God, and thus also with one another. The fact that each child partakes in the spirit is also an intrinsic part of our human nature and our Christianity when we are adults.

Turning to childhood does not have to mean that we only look back to biographical beginnings. Christ describes the developmental ideal in terms of Christians becoming childlike in relation to the future: 'Truly I tell you, unless you change and become like little children, you will never enter the kingdom of heaven' (Matt. 18:3). What comes to expression as spiritual yearning in the night-time question posed by Nicodemus is something which the poet Novalis puts as follows in one of his Fragments: 'Every stage of education starts with childhood. That is why the most refined and cultured earthly human being so closely resembles the child.' All social initiatives that look to the value of a 'simple life' and its sustainability – whether it be the renunciation of an economic compulsion to 'produce' as urged by Byung-Chul Han, or the non-goal-oriented but deeply meaningful playfulness described by Friedrich Schiller – can be seen and realised as religious seeds.[3] Immediacy of devotion, unconditional love, openness and mobility of perceptions, are only a few exemplary qualities of childhood that contribute and sustain community amongst Christians.

3.

Confirmation: Dismissed into Life

Unlike the Church's narrow view in medieval times of the need to renounce the earthly world, Christian communities today, trusting fully in God's engagement with the world, can reflect the fact that resurrection and eternal life in Christ are promised not only to humanity, but to the whole of creation. We should not teach and model earthly renunciation to young people. Instead, we should encourage them and each other to cultivate short periods of contemplation so that, by permeating the world with spirit, can make such spiritualisation fruitful.

The relationship between religion and life

Amongst the less fruitful Christian traditions is the fact that the Church sees itself as a kind of moral authority in society, a counter-pole to mundane human life. An old joke highlights this:

A man came home from church.
'What was the sermon today?' his wife asked.
'It was about sin,' the man replied.
'Yes, but what did the priest say about it?'
'He said he was against it,' the man said.

Anyone nowadays who preaches an ethical stance based on the avoidance of mistakes rather than seeing them as presenting opportunities to learn, is at risk of cutting themselves off from their fellow human beings and from real life. Moral 'purity', principally characterised by a certain distance from life, loses contact with the rich and nuanced realms of existence that arise only from continually rediscovering an ethical balance between limited outlooks of diverse kinds.

In the sacrament of baptism in The Christian Community it is said that the soul of the child has been sent down 'from the community of spirit to that of the earth'. This might initially sound as though the spiritual world and the earthly world stand in contrast or opposition to one another. But the text goes on to say that we should receive the soul as a 'congregation gathered for this baptism' and bear it into 'the communion of the Christ Jesus'. In other words, although the congregation is an earthly community, it sees itself at the same time as a spiritual community gathered together in the name of Jesus Christ. Christianity does not seek to divide spirit and the earth but to unite them.

The second sacrament in the life of a baptised person now aims to reassert or *confirm* this. During confirmation we hear the words, 'With concern in my soul I dismiss you now into life.' This does not mean that we give children up for lost, but rather that we see their future life as being deeply connected with the sacrament we are together celebrating. Rather than marking an end of the influence of religion, in the sacrament of confirmation we celebrate its continual working and its expansion to encompass the life of adolescents in the world.

Members of a Christian community that closes itself off from the wider world are open to the charge of cultivating religious egoism: of being concerned only with their own salvation while ignoring the welfare of their fellow human beings. Non-members will feel little inclination to engage with them let alone join them. Rather, a sense will arise that such a 'closed society' is trying to raise itself above the rest of the world, which begs the question whether such a community can still be called 'Christian'. When Christ sent his apostles out into the world, the mission he entrusted them with spoke of a union between heaven and earth on the one hand, and the apostles and their fellow human beings on the other:

> All authority in heaven and on earth has been
> given to me. Therefore go and make disciples
> of all nations, baptising them in the name of

the Father and of the Son and of the Holy
Spirit, and teaching them to obey everything
I have commanded you. And surely I am with
you always, to the very end of the age. (Matt.
28:18–20)

Sent out into the world

While the performing of every sacrament calls us away from
the world for a short while (the Greek word for Christian
community is *ekklesia*, which originally means a gathering
of the people summoned by the herald), nevertheless, at the
end of every such act of celebration, we become apostles,
people sent out into the world with a religious initiative.
This dual movement – of turning inwards for a while
before going outwards – also lies in the word 'deliver': in
connection with birth it refers to a mother being 'delivered'
of her child. The transition from one mode of existence to
another means being 'unbound' or delivered from one set of
circumstances and incorporated into a new one. Our first
delivery and incorporation into the world at birth is followed
by many further biographical stages in which delivery and
reintegration must be accomplished both by parents and
their child: parents must allow themselves to be 'delivered' of
their child, actively releasing them or unbinding them into
their own existence.

We find words corresponding to this in the Gospel of John following the raising of Lazarus. After Jesus has called and awoken him from the grave into new life with the words, 'Lazarus, come out!' (John 11:43), he says to those standing around, 'Take off the grave cloths and let him go' (John 1:44). First he must be unbound from the cloths that have wrapped the corpse, and then he can be released into life again. The Greek word for 'release' is *aphiemi*, and besides 'letting go' it can also mean a person is relieved of their guilt or debts in the sense of 'forgiveness'. This word figures twice more in the further course of John's Gospel. The first time is during the 'Farewell Discourses' after the Last Supper with the disciples: 'Peace I leave with you; my peace I give you. I do not give to you as the world gives' (John 14:27). What Jesus bequeaths or delivers to his own is the power of peace that is bound up with his being. This is reiterated in the Act of Consecration of the Human Being: 'I stand at peace with the world.' The second recurrence of *aphiemi* comes in the account of the appearance of the resurrected one on the evening of Easter day. After greeting them with the words of peace, and breathing upon them to fill them with spirit, he finally says to the disciples, 'If you forgive anyone's sins, their sins are forgiven; if you do not forgive them, they are not forgiven' (John 20:23). Thus, as a priestly mission given to the apostles, alongside the giving of peace, comes an empowerment to heal the sickness of sin.[1] In this sense, all believers can feel called upon to direct their religious practice and actions toward their human brothers and sisters and toward the life of the world.

What we as Christians can release into life

When we let confirmands go, releasing them into the world and their own lives, our 'solicitous soul' can perceive and evaluate what this generation is able to contribute out of its own spiritual impulses to the further development of our culture. But this still holds true of the religious life of older members of the congregation. How can they benefit humanity as Christians? Surely it is in this way: that first and foremost, despite the uncertainty of their faith, they are striving to acknowledge the presence of God in the world. They are growing more awake to signs of Christ's return in our time and are seeking to draw upon his world-transformative power in order to work for peace, love and life. In this way, older members can also feel connected with young people whom, at Confirmation, we have blessed with the words of release.

4.

Communion: Becoming One Body

At the Last Supper the need to eat became the central focus of Christian community-building. We can see this as a hopeful sign of how Christ's healing work seeks to enliven the future of human community. But the fact that we need one another in order to develop and progress appears here only as an initial spur. Only when we take this up in conscious freedom and unfold it further does it create nourishment for souls who find one another in all-embracing fellowship as the body of Christ.

Celebrating life and community

Human responsibility for the garden of Paradise, and permission to eat of all other trees, was implicit in our eating the forbidden fruit of the Tree of the Knowledge of Good and Evil:

> The Lord God took the man and put him in the
> Garden of Eden to work it and take care of it. And
> the Lord God commanded the man, 'You are
> free to eat from any tree in the garden; but you
> must not eat from the Tree of the Knowledge of
> Good and Evil, for when you eat from it you will
> certainly die.' (Gen. 2:15–17)

The primordial human couple were therefore the first table fellowship, but by transgressing the divine commandment and eating from the forbidden tree, they tragically entered a fellowship of mortality as well. This denotes two very different dimensions of communal eating, which have also determined the Judaeo-Christian history of the sanctified meal. First, our body cannot survive on its own but needs earthly food to sustain it. Second, just as through our sense perception and our breathing we are shown to be an 'open system' in reciprocal relationship with our surroundings, so, too, through the food we ingest, we become subject to the 'life and death' of the world, bound up with it and with our fellow human beings. Religion acknowledges and blesses the natural necessity involved in the meal, but at the same time it looks beyond mere survival and celebrates a renewal of life and community through the rites and rituals of this shared experience.

The threatening proximity of death and the protection against it play an important role in the origins of the Jewish

Passover feast: the doorposts of the house of every table fellowship were to be daubed with the blood of the sacrificial lamb, as a sign to the angel of death that it should pass by that dwelling.[1] At the meal held on the eve of the flight from Egypt, however, the emphasis was first and foremost on the promise and affirmation of the future community of the Israelites as God's chosen people in the promised land. In this context, the Christian Last Supper also directly connects life and death: on Maundy Thursday, Christ utters his farewell to his disciples in a distinctive Passover feast. He looks ahead to his death on the cross and connects this unique moment with the promise of his immanent presence in the sign of the sacred meal of bread and wine. He offers himself up as the sacrifice from which will arise a living community between him and the celebrants who eat the bread and drink the wine that have become his body and blood. Wherever we enact this sign, we seek community with the overcomer of death, and, rather than receiving mortal substance, instead receive through the resurrection of Christ the eternal life that he has promised to all those who unite with him in faith: 'I am the resurrection and the life. The one who believes in me will live, even though they die' (John 11:25).

Death and life do not have to be seen as irreconcilable opposites, but together can be understood as part of a more comprehensive process, one that can help earthly existence gain an entirely different quality. The path leading from life to death and thence to new life from death does not run in a linear fashion, but points to the transformation of life through death, and of death through life. With resurrection we are not called back into our old life but into a new one that bursts the bounds of space and time. The phrase 'eternal life' occurs here, and Christ goes on to speak of this when he says '…and whoever lives by believing in me will never die' (John 11:26).[2]

Not divided but united

If, instead of seeing the world as divided by such absolute polarities as life and death, humanity and God, time and eternity, we understand it in terms of dynamic processes, we can begin to recognise that in the central Christian sacrament of communion we are not sanctifying a single biographical moment, but ever and anew the daily moment of eating. Christ does not choose any particular food as the bearer of his immanent presence but ordinary 'fruits from every tree'. The natural necessity of eating is transformed into the living process of the new presence of the creator God within his creation. What was sundered at the end of the drama of Paradise is to be reunited through the symbolic deed of the Last Supper in collaborative interplay between humanity and God.

The meaning of transubstantiation poses a challenge to those who do not wish to simply accept the miraculous sanctification of substance, but who instead seek to develop a thinking that can comprehend this enactment.[3] A key to such thinking lies in the exercise of trying to discern things from different perspectives. By strengthening our power of reason in this way and connecting diverse approaches with one another, we create the possibility of gaining insight into what we are studying.

In the case of our understanding of communion this can mean the following: instead of wondering whether what we ingest is bread *or* the body of Christ, whether it is wine *or* Christ's blood, what matters, rather, is whether we find a way to think both thoughts in full accord. Can the mundane be at the same time miraculous? Can the profane be at the same time sacred? Can the divine be, or become, at the same time human? If, after many attempts, this question can be answered ever more strongly in the affirmative, then our Christianity as a whole can shift from the 'exceptional place' in which it has languished – for whatever reason – at various phases of our cultural history.

'Now you are the body of Christ'

This way of thinking corresponds to a form of community-building addressed by the apostle Paul in the picture of the congregation as the body of Christ: 'Now you are the body of Christ, and each one of you is a part of it' (1 Cor. 12:27).

From this it becomes apparent that such a community in Christ does not arise through the addition of uniform units; rather, it grows and lives as an organic whole composed of diverse yet interrelating parts.[4] In the context of eating, an invisible and delicate form of this corporeality arises in a seemingly paradoxical way: if the table fellowship of the Last Supper is seen as an active one in so far as those present take in the body and blood of Christ, from another perspective this 'eating' means that the community is at the same time absorbed and taken up by the resurrected one. They are integrated into the living fabric of his body. This two-way dynamic of Christian community-building can encourage us in all kinds of initiatives, including that of allowing daily life and every kind of human encounter to be, in the sense of a 'feeding' occurrence, the seed for further transformation.

5.

Consultation: Remembrance and Renewal

The sacrament of confession, known as sacramental consultation in The Christian Community, has to do with an act of personal transformation. At the same time, it is central to the development of community: what connects us to our origins should be maintained, but there should also be a renewal through a spirit of modernity that looks ahead to the future. It seems fitting that the great transformation in the history of the Church, the Reformation, was sparked by a dispute about the sacrament of confession.

Christianity as both mystical and actual

In 1929, the German theologian Dietrich Bonhoeffer wrote: 'A God who "exists" does not exist.'[1] If we think of the Christian God as a Trinity in evolution, he can never be fixed as a simple fact. God is, for us, both the ground of all creation and the dynamic principle in it. Every encounter of the soul with him will initially be of an inwardly mystical kind, but it also relates to the fact of Jesus Christ becoming man and overcoming death at the turning point of time. What can arise and grow in such encounters is the receptive and creative power of faith – a mystical-actual reality. The Greek word for believe, *pisteuein*, can be heard as active trust, as intimate relationship with the divine that proceeds from the encounter of an open heart with the divine being who is willing to take up habitation in the human being.

At the beginning of the third Christian millennium, the experiences we gain through engagement with the Bible acquire more importance than the question of its historical certainty. By immersing ourselves in the words and images of the gospel, our soul can experience an active stream of life that raises us into the sphere of the divine Word of the Creator and can nourish us at a deep level of our being. In it lives what Christ promised his disciples as they looked upon the temple at Jerusalem: 'Heaven and earth will pass away but my words will not pass away' (Luke 21:33). In 1902, Rudolf Steiner gave the lectures that formed *Christianity as Mystical Fact* out of this kind of deep contemplation. In them he founded an anthroposophic Christology, which he subsequently developed throughout the rest of his writing and lecturing career. Peter Selg writes that this was 'a free, remembrance-type access out of his own I to events at and around Golgotha'.[2]

In his view of the effect of archetypal images, the psychoanalyst Carl Gustav Jung thought that individuals might potentially have such 'remembrance-type' access (albeit non-active) to supra-individual ideas and their ongoing influence. According to him, the archetype is 'not only a picture as such but at the same time also a dynamic force announcing itself in numinosity, in the power of fascination of the archetypal image'.[3]

But let us return to the comment by Bonhoeffer we quoted at the outset. The existence of God, from the human perspective, is not accessible at the level of facts – at least he does not 'exist' there as such. But in mystic experience of belief we can certainly become aware of the presence of God and his creative powers, and from this intimate stratum of experience acknowledge the reality of Biblical contents and also of the incarnation and resurrection of Christ. Believers can notice that they actively contribute to the efficacy of God in the world of actualities.

Integrating time as a way of life

When we take responsibility for our life, we experience our relationship to the past and the future as a tension between mystical and actual dimensions. Remembering is a mystical act: it connects us anew each time with what we can bring into the present from what has gone before, which signifies more than just 'learning from the past'. By integrating what we have experienced into our present life, we do not simply repeat what has been, but at the same time undertake a creative act. We raise something out of its dead state, recreate it, and allow it to affect and shape our future life. In this way we can give a new and possibly deeper meaning to our past experiences.

In the parable of the Prodigal Son such a memory is presented as a religious conversion: 'When he came to his senses, he said, "How many of my father's hired servants have food to spare, and here I am starving to death! I will set out and go back to my father"' (Luke 15:17–18). The son has not yet set out on the journey to his father, but inwardly he forms the intention that he then seeks to realise outwardly. The further narrative then traces how the I draws the future into the present in what Wolfgang Schad calls 'time-integration'.[4]

Bringing the past and future to life through the practice of time integration can be seen as the central process of a contemporary sacrament of confession, or sacramental consultation: I look back in contemplation and in doing so experience a transformed relationship with myself; I then open my gaze to what has hitherto lain beyond my horizon and is waiting to be discovered by me.[5] In daily life, we can experience this transition from simple memory to religious activity whenever people talk about aspects of their biography. This can be further intensified if these life memories go beyond an account of successes and sufferings to reveal the individual who, through both successes and failures, feels gratitude for their path of development and those who have played a part in it.

Shared memorials create presence of mind

Two aspects of a contemporary culture of memory come to mind in considering how religious community-building can develop out of the spirit of the sacramental consultation. In public memorials that sometimes follow tragic events, periods of silence are often observed. Such invitations to reflect together on what has been experienced creates a sense of community without imposing on each individual present the will of those who speak. Something else that comes to expression here is how a sense of social responsibility for the consequences of the event being commemorated becomes still more meaningful if it breaks through the barriers between generations: community-building always presents us with a perspective of time that goes beyond each individual's lifespan.

In founding the sacramental life, Christ speaks of the principle of 'remembering by name' when he says, as he breaks the bread, 'Do this in remembrance of me' (Luke 22:19 and 1 Cor. 11:24). In the original Greek, the word *anámnesis* is used here, which can also be translated as 'memory' or 'bringing to mind'. Accordingly, Christian community-building can be understood as something that not only reminds us of divine influence in history, but that also calls God himself into communities. In memory, we recall what became historical fact at the founding of Christianity through a divine deed, but at the same time we also develop an awareness of that presence which seeks to become active in our midst both today and in the future.

6.

Marriage: An Enhancement of Life's Potential

Rather than fearing difference in its members, communities should experience the richness in this and the potential for creative diversity. The key to this wealth lies in a willingness to embrace the potential of polarities. In this context, the sacrament of Christian marriage should be seen as a celebration of the potential that can unfold in the interplay between two different people. At work here is one of the fundamental principles of human community-building.

Diversity as a creative principle

As a result of polarities, the world as creation is composed of multiple unique beings, rather than uniform entities emerging from some mechanical reproduction. In the Christian view, life is endowed with its origins, movement and meaning by the divine subjects of Father, Son and Holy

Spirit. The threefold God indwells it and is active within it.

One of life's productive polarities is the duality of masculine and feminine. As we read at the beginning of Genesis, the first human being was already placed into this polarity before the division of the sexes:

> So God created mankind in his own image, in the
> image of God he created them; male and female he
> created them. (Gen, 1:27)

That we incarnate one-sidedly as either male or female does not have to be seen as being limiting, but can instead be acknowledged as the beginning of each person's self-creating power. We are not fixed, either in a particular way of being human or in terms of being oriented towards a uniform and predetermined goal. Over and against the physical gender assigned to us at birth, stands the soul-spiritual counter-pole of the other gender, which is concealed yet active within us. Rudolf Steiner impressed on the founders of The Christian Community an understanding of the sacrament of marriage as something that should serve the consecration of this polarity in every human being.[1] Differing qualities can be experienced as a creative potential that opens up a wealth of possible ways to be human. Successful marriage partnerships do not emerge from the attempt to harmonise with one another in a uniform way, but arise, rather, from the partners experiencing both individuation and community-building: a diversity of configurations and changes that nevertheless point equally to the image of God within us.

Unfolding potential

According to the neurobiologist Gerald Hüther, it is time we moved away from the conception of community-building as a mere exchange of resources, towards one that sees commonality as fruitful only when we help each other to mature and unfold our potential:

> No one can unfold the potential inherent in them,
> their talents and gifts, when they are treated as
> object and not as subject, when they do not feel
> themselves respected and esteemed.[2]

This perspective is associated with a new view of I development. The shared life of individuals and communities cannot be enhanced by the ego asserting itself at the expense of others, but only by the mature I that is at work in the unfolding of potential. Each person can facilitate the other. In the Epistle to the Philippians, Paul presents as an example of this the devotion with which Christ relinquished his divine nature:

Do nothing out of selfish ambition or vain
conceit. Rather, in humility value others above
yourselves, not looking to your own interests but each
of you to the interests of the others. (Phil. 2:3–4)

The history of the Christian Church shows few examples of mutual respect of differing views. Following unification under the Roman Emperor, it has been marked by an ongoing series of exclusions and divisions. Only in the twentieth century, with the Ecumenical movement, did an initiative arise that reversed this trend. Perhaps in interreligious dialogue (say between Jews, Muslims and Christians) it will become easier to engage with differences, since we can experience them as helpful in the unfolding of our own potential. This is something that all communities of different and differing people can strive for.

Community with otherness

In the marriage sacrament of The Christian Community, a blessing is given upon the marrying couple's resolve to create a 'community of life'.[3] This way of defining marriage refers to two interrelated conditions of the desired partnership: a true togetherness that is more than just two people living with each other, and the support and encouragement of each other as each partner continues to develop. The marriage sacrament can also apply to Christian communities in this sense: that the members of such congregations can and should repeatedly become strangers to one another so as to rediscover each other and what connects them.

The blessing that concludes the words of the marriage service shows how encompassing such community can be in its source and origin, in its presence and its goals: it speaks of how souls have come from 'worlds of God', and thus the foundations of their human existence are rooted in their God-likeness. It says also that 'They have found one another in earth existence,' pointing both to the fact that they first found each other, but then also to their intention to rediscover each other anew whenever they lose sight of one another. In a third step, the words express how the shared soul forces of the marriage partners should receive the blessing of the threefold God in 'light of spirit, warmth of soul and inwardness of heart'. Three phrases are here named that can astonish us: earth thinking, earth feeling and earth will. This sounds as if, with divine succour, a special task is laid upon the common soul of the marriage, one that far surpasses the two individuals concerned as well as the community celebrating the marriage with them. What communities of this kind unfold as human potential is to benefit the entirety of the earth's being, for their fellowship is founded in the spirit of God, is resolved upon ever and anew by the I, and aims for the great nuptial goal of the 're-enlivening of the dying earth existence'.[4]

7.

Ordination: A Priestly Siblinghood

Part of the tragedy of ecclesiastical history has been an over-emphasis on the authority of priests. The fundamental stance of Christianity does not imply a dominance of the initiated over other believers, but rather a mutual respect for the diversity of gifts and tasks in the community of brothers and sisters. The sacrament of ordination can therefore become a sign of the active faith and mutual service from which true fellowship among Christians proceeds.

God-affinity: the origins and future of humanity

Carl Jung once formulated the basic question of religion in this way: 'The decisive question for man is: Is he related to something infinite or not? That is the telling question of his life.'[1] This is not about whether we recognise or acknowledge a personal God, whether we obey his commandments or seek his succour and aid. Rather, the subtle choice of words points initially to whether we seek within our being for a bridge from the familiar finite world to an infinite one. Job, one of the great figures of suffering in the Hebrew Bible, expressed as follows his relationship with the infinite being of God:

> Naked I came from my mother's womb, and naked
> I will depart. The Lord gave and the Lord has taken
> away; may the name of the Lord be praised.
> (Job 1:21)

The apostle Paul speaks to the Athenians about humanity's affinity with God in quite different terms:

> The God who made the world and everything in
> it is the Lord of heaven and earth and does not live
> in temples built by human hands. And he is not
> served by human hands, as if he needed anything.
> Rather, he himself gives everyone life and breath
> and everything else. From one man he made all the
> nations, that they should inhabit the whole earth;
> and he marked out their appointed times in history
> and the boundaries of their lands. God did this so
> that they would seek him and perhaps reach out for
> him and find him, though he is not far from any

one of us. 'For in him we live and move and have
our being.' As some of your own poets have said,
'We are his offspring.' (Acts 17:24–28)

God no longer appears here as a distant figure, as
commanding Lord over birth and death, but as an infinite
being who takes up habitation in the finite world: we live
in him, move within him and feel our being raised up in his
being. Paul is not speaking here of a more or less unreachable
deity whom the human being must obey, but of one who
is close and in no way distant from us. Even if, like Job,
we perhaps have no direct experience of God during our
earthly lifetime, according to Paul we nevertheless have an
inner path of seeking, sensing and finding. The three verses
of the Trinitarian opening and closing prayer of the Act of
Consecration of the Human Being refer to such an approach
in speaking three times of 'feeling our way towards' God:
God the Father 'conscious of our humanity', God the Son
'aware of the Christ', and the healing God 'grasping the
spirit'.

The first words for the ordination of priests in The
Christian Community allow us to perceive this sacrament
as an active relationship with the infinite nature of the being
of God. The deity is here called the 'eternal ground of all
transient existence'. In full accord with the words of Paul
quoted above, this is followed by the words, 'You, Being of

all that is.' What now comes no longer sounds as if it refers only to God the Father. After the next line, 'Devoted to Your will,' the text continues with 'waiting for Your light'. After this address to the future, the prayer ends finally by saying, 'We draw near to You'. The community of those wishing to participate in the ordination of candidates called from their midst, approach the one whose return they long for. With this approach the people uttering this prayer relate themselves to both aspects of their affinity with God: they wish to find the origin and goal of their human existence in God, and also to learn, live and work out of it.[2]

Belief as priestly power

In October 1921, Rudolf Steiner impressed on those who were to found The Christian Community a connection between affinity, or relatedness, and the power of belief:

> Belief means finding in one's soul such a strength
> and force directed towards Christ that this soul
> strength, this soul force becomes as great as that
> which blood bonds can elicit in us. Then we find
> the way to the unitary Christ of all humanity,
> that unitary Christ who, through the event of
> Golgotha, is also the truly objective cause of every
> subjective process of redemption.[3]

The word 'affinity' comes via the Old French *afinite* (meaning 'relationship' or 'kinship' but also 'neighbourhood' or 'vicinity') from the Latin *affinis*, meaning 'adjoining, adjacent', literally 'bordering on'. But in modern English, 'feeling an affinity' with something or someone implies a seeking of connection that is much more active than a 'given' blood relationship or natural adjacency. With the title of his novel *Elective Affinities*, Goethe coined a phrase that suggests going beyond blood relationships in our resolve to approach others and make them into our 'relations'.

We can see the connection of Christians with Christ at communion as being an 'elective affinity' of this kind, one celebrated in the mystery of Christ's body and blood. At the beginning of the Last Supper, Jesus also founds a community based on a fellowship of equals:

> I no longer call you servants, because a servant
> does not know his master's business. Instead,
> I have called you friends, for everything that I
> learned from my Father I have made known to
> you. (John 15:15)

Before the entry into Jerusalem, he had proclaimed to the disciples a reversed hierarchy in the community of Christians, affirmed by the ritual of the washing of the feet:

You know that the rulers of the Gentiles lord
it over them, and their high officials exercise
authority over them. Not so with you. Instead,
whoever wants to become great among you must
be your servant, and whoever wants to be first
must be your slave – just as the Son of Man did
not come to be served, but to serve, and to give his
life as a ransom for many. (Matt. 20:25–28)

The ordination of priests is not the beginning of the God-affinity of those ordained but a celebration, associated with a deep resolve, to repeatedly and lastingly be connected with the task of serving God's 'Word-presiding wisdom', and to become caretaker of his 'world-healing sway'.

Religious renewal through priestly life

Seeing belief as a priestly power of God-connectedness in all believers corresponds to a view of active religious life that is not limited to the traditional domain of the Church. For the past hundred years now, the life of The Christian Community has been connected with a longing for 'religious renewal', and this can certainly be regarded as an encompassing cultural initiative arising from the wellspring of Christian religiosity. Just as we can pursue this goal through the sacraments and the active life of Christian congregations, so too can we through personal devoutness and the leading of a Christian life. Over and above this, it is possible for believers to practise cultural engagement in all social realms, and this may be still more desired and necessary than we think. Religious community-building nowadays cannot limit itself to self-involvement but only truly follows Christ when Christian thinking, feeling and action are made fruitful for the renewal of culture and civilisation.

8.

Community in Christ

As far back as the time of the apostles, understanding of community in a Christian sense has been founded on the idea that, alongside the inner configuration of the divine Trinity itself, the Christ being is connected with the congregation who belongs to him. This is the Pauline picture of the congregation as the body of Christ. In this chapter we will explore this unique annunciation of God's future fellowship with human beings.

The being and body of Christ

The question of God's grandeur is one of the most fundamental religious issues. Even if Christians see the Son of God as a God who is made intimately close to us through his incarnation in Jesus, the nature of the Trinity itself remains a scarcely comprehensible mystery. To see Father, Son and Spirit as a threefold *and* three-in-one figure is a challenge to both belief and understanding. Added to this, Paul proclaims that the members of the church community are part of the body of Christ, in which the baptised find themselves as limbs of Christ's body (Eph. 1:23). The third quality of divine corporeality arises from Jesus Christ's special connectedness with the earth. What is achieved and accomplished in Christ's passage through death and its overcoming at the resurrection not only seeks to redeem human beings from their bonds of transience and perishability, but also to liberate the whole of creation. This becomes apparent in Chapter 8 of Paul's Epistle to the Romans.

What then must we regard as the body of Christ?

Is it his unity with God the Father and the Holy Spirit in the encompassing being of the Trinity? Is it his deep connection with Christians as the head of the body of which the congregations and the faithful are the limbs? Or did the earthly world become his body as he passed through Easter and Ascension?

Here we make no progress with static concepts and pictures. The Trinity cannot separate itself from the evolving world and human beings as they pass through alienation from God to redemption. To this also belongs the connection of the Father, Son and Spirit to the nine hierarchies of angels, a perspective that expands our view of the cosmic scope and grandeur of the Trinity. If we give serious credence to the relationship that Christ enters into at the Last Supper with the earthly gifts of bread and wine, then the being of the earth can just as equally be seen as his corporeality. From this it follows that the diverse dimensions within which Christ lives and is present cannot be a matter of either/or, but rather of all-at-once. If Christ's body is composed of God, the congregation of the faithful, and the earth itself, this is surely only possible because his being encompasses both heaven and earth.

The congregation as the body of Christ

In relation to those baptised in Christ, Paul employs the image of the congregation as Christ's body, at the same time heralding this as a reality: 'Now you are the body of Christ, and each one of you is a part of it' (1 Cor. 12:27). He begins these teachings with a view of the various ways in which Christian life can develop. The Greek words *chárisma* (endowment by grace) and *diakonía* (service), which he employs here, characterise the interplay between gifts endowed by the spirit and the willingness of human beings to make these gifts effective in the world. Fundamentally, religious deeds are accomplished through the receptivity of hearts and the active longing for work:

> Now to each one the manifestation of the Spirit
> is given for the common good. To one there is

given through the Spirit a message of wisdom, to
another a message of knowledge by means of
the same Spirit, to another faith by the same
Spirit, to another gifts of healing by that one
Spirit, to another miraculous powers, to another
prophecy, to another distinguishing between
spirits, to another speaking in different kinds of
tongues, and to still another the interpretation
of tongues. All these are the work of one and the
same Spirit, and he distributes them to each one,
just as he determines. Just as a body, though one,
has many parts, but all its many parts form one
body, so it is with Christ. (1 Cor. 12:8–12)

What at first glance appears to the reader as an
overwhelming multiplicity of spiritual dimensions and
practices, receives, in the following verses, a beneficially
ordering overview. In his office as spiritual teacher of the
congregation, Paul here develops a grandiose, pictorial
lecture on communal interplay. The author shows how the
parts of the body communicate with each other, pointing to
the mutual esteem necessary for community-building:

Now if the foot should say, 'Because I am not a
hand, I do not belong to the body,' it would not
for that reason stop being part of the body. And

> if the ear should say, 'Because I am not an eye, I
> do not belong to the body,' it would not for that
> reason stop being part of the body. If the whole
> body were an eye, where would the sense of
> hearing be? If the whole body were an ear, where
> would the sense of smell be? But in fact God has
> placed the parts in the body, every one of them,
> just as he wanted them to be. If they were all one
> part, where would the body be? As it is, there are
> many parts, but one body. (1 Cor. 12:15–20)

With pastoral sensibility, the apostle here first addresses potentially unsure members of his flock, who, in their particular nature, may not feel themselves to be welcome in the congregation. Next he turns to those who might take offence at the otherness of 'alien' parts of the community or who might be inclined to take a judgemental attitude of others:

> The eye cannot say to the hand, 'I don't need you!'
> And the head cannot say to the feet, 'I don't need
> you!' On the contrary, those parts of the body
> that seem to be weaker are indispensable, and
> the parts that we think are less honourable
> we treat with special honour. And the parts
> that are unpresentable are treated with special

modesty, while our presentable parts need no special treatment. But God has put the body together, giving greater honour to the parts that lacked it, so that there should be no division in the body, but that its parts should have equal concern for each other. (1 Cor. 12:21–25)

Organic community building

The skin is regarded as the largest organ of the human body, simultaneously dividing and connecting different parts of our anatomy. It protects what belongs to it and at the same time creates permeability for things outside it. It also possesses an extraordinarily encompassing and rapid capacity for regeneration: roughly every thirty days the surface of our body renews itself entirely, the skin within being younger while its ageing becomes apparent on its outward surface.

Paul's picture of the body and its parts can be applied to social and community-building processes in the organism of the parish or congregation. There, too, many different regulatory and configuring tasks exist for the benefit of the social organism as a whole: privacy and transparency, cooperation and division of labour, the maturity of age and the youthful power of renewal, and so on. The principles of inclusion and exclusion have dramatically informed the history of Christian community-building: who belongs to the congregation, who does not, and who gets to determine this? It would be fascinating to examine the organism's diverse functional systems in terms of their tangible relevance to, or correspondence with, the life of a community.

One thing would certainly come to light: that without each other we cannot exist, nor can we bring about what becomes possible in and through the connection with the Christ being as union of the human and the divine.

9.

Celebrating Life

Can a study of the various qualities of the Christian sacraments provide us with different perspectives on the theme of community-building? With this question in mind, the attempt has been made in this book not to describe the life of twenty-first-century Christian congregations as a given, let alone a uniform organisational structure, but as a many and varied instance of spiritual development through communality. According to this view, Christ is less an historical initiator than a living spirit who, from the sphere of the divine, accompanies and fulfils what human beings undertake together as they draw closer to him. Christian religious actions, already in their Old Testament roots, do not so much signify 'weekly work' as celebration – a celebration of life with God as the source of strength for human actions in daily life. The following seven aspects of such celebration are characterised below.

In death and resurrection

Turning our gaze towards life when threatened by illness and death does not have to mean an avoidance and disregard of suffering and dying, nor a despairing search for solace. Instead, it can be celebrated as the beginning of a more encompassing view of life. If we wish to overcome death, we should not push it away from us but accept it and its transformative potential. 'I am the rebirth in death, I am the life in dying,' is how the burial rite reproduces the words of Christ (John 11:25). For the community this means that everything which seemingly separates and divides us can be the beginning of a deeper connection. All loss can lead to renewal. The cross as the central symbol of Christianity unites dying with the beginning of true life.

In receiving and nurturing

Life is always a gift; it cannot be produced or allocated, but requires service and care if it is to thrive. That is what children teach their parents who, in the sacrament of baptism, can become conscious of the fact that through receiving and nurturing newly incarnating souls they are also touched by the tender ties of the spirit. Wherever the creative power of what comes to earth brings us together, we become witnesses and way-preparers of the new. 'May you lead this soul, that he/she may be, grow, become in

70

the Christ-community,' are the words uttered at the baptismal celebration. All spiritual communities have their roots in heaven, their branches, leaves and fruits growing earthwards. Their seeds seek to grow in human beings who together receive them and give them space to continue unfolding their vitality.

In blessing and dismissing

The goal of increasing self-determination takes a further step towards realisation when children cross the threshold into adolescence. We celebrate this in the sacrament of confirmation: 'So let Your blessing stream at this hour on those who are entrusted to us,' is what we beseech of Christ at the beginning, and we dismiss the children with 'concern in my soul' into life. That a spiritual potential lies in dismissing or letting go is already apparent in the Creator's first gesture as he lets his creatures go forth from himself. What communities seek to accomplish for outsiders and the world can only come to effect if we take our farewell from them in the spirit of blessing, knowing well that original connections will never be lost entirely.

In transforming and uniting

In the sacrament of communion we approach the heart of religious life. We experience the heartbeat that weaves together centre and periphery, faithfulness and transformation, the opening I of those present and the self-giving I of divine presence. With the promise, 'Take me forasmuch as you have given yourself to me,' we receive Christ into us and amongst us in the Act of Consecration of the Human Being. Having celebrated this union of heaven and earth, the community then returns to its tasks in a spirit of devotion and giving, bearing within it the impulse of peace that it has received.

In remembering and renewing

Another aspect of I-culture lies in a willingness to repeatedly examine and take issue with what we have become in life. Tranquil contemplation of the soul's memory pictures is the ground upon which the strength to change grows. Each time I reflect upon who I have been, I can become aware of who I wish to become. Whenever we cast our gaze backwards, we are already engaging in transformation and, in the sacramental consultation, can accept these words: 'You will find wonder and love for the revelation of God and prove yourself full of love for human beings.' Community does not arise purely out of the shared interests that bring people together in pursuit of a common goal, but also from a willingness to actively develop the old from the past into the new that serves the future.

In unity and diversity

In the sacrament of marriage, we hear: 'From worlds of God your souls have come; they have found one another in earth existence.' Every kind of community-building, not only a life partnership, is accomplished under this guiding star. Finding other people as the foundation of a shared life is always the rediscovery of existing ties and connections within the creative spirit.

In word and deed

We human beings, with our priestly potential, find ourselves in life at a threshold between the sacred and profane: as servants of the divine message that can come forth from hidden regions in every human word, and as caretakers of the deeds of God that can enable all human deeds to become signs of the workings of the spirit in the world. 'Wherever you go, Christ walks with you,' are the words of the festive covenant uttered at the ordination of priests, who henceforth wish to unite their life with the office of priest in service to a community. To acknowledge freely and with courageous spirit that the presence of God is in everything mundane yet remains continually inaccessible, is something that can also encompass the spiritual aspect of human co-existence. The spirit of a community can develop priestly qualities.

Community-building discerned in this way through the sacraments cannot – or at least not any longer – be derived from specific divine commandments. It can only come from the sovereign resolves of each individual to participate in open mutuality. Such resolves naturally require an open and unconditional invitation to God to turn towards this community of separate individuals.

Notes

Introduction
1. See Nancy, Jean-Luc, *Re-treating Religion: Deconstructing Christianity with Jean-Luc Nancy (Perspectives in Continental Philosophy)*, Fordham University Press, USA 2012.
2. Pohl-Patalong, Uta, *Bibel Lesen. Die Kraft der heiligen Texte* [Reading the Bible: The Power of the Sacred Texts], Freiburg, Germany 2010.
3. Steiner, Rudolf, *Social and Antisocial Forces in the Human Being*, Mercury Press, USA 1982.
4. Bonhoeffer, Dietrich, *Life Together*, 1517 Media, USA 2015.

1. Anointing: The Art of Dying
1. Arendt, Hannah, *The Human Condition*, University of Chicago Press, USA 2018.
2. Matthias Claudius was an essayist who wrote the words of the poem 'Death and the Maiden', which Schubert later put to music.
3. *The Art of Dying* consists of two Latin texts from the fifteenth century that give advice on how to 'die well'.

2. Baptism: A Festival of Recognition
1. Hesse, Hermann, 'Stufen' in *Sämtliche Gedichte in einem Band* [All Poems in One Volume], Insel Verlag, Germany 1995.
2. Han, Byung-Chul, *Vom Verschwinden der Rituale. Eine Topologie*

der Gegenwart [The Disappearance of Rituals: A Topology of the Present], Ullstein Verlag, Germany 2019.

3. See Hüther, Gerald and Quarch, Christoph, *Rettet das Spiel! Weil Leben mehr als Funktionieren ist* [Save the Game! Because Life is More than Functioning], Hanser Verlag, Germany 2016.

3. Confirmation: Dismissed into Life

1. See Meier, Ulrich, *Die Beichte. Atem der Liebe – das Sakrament der Menschwerdung* [Confession: Breath of Love – the Sacrament of the Incarnation], Urachhaus, Germany 2019, p. 60ff.

4. Communion: Becoming One Body

1. See Exodus, Chapter 12.
2. See Meier, Ulrich, 'nicht zum Tode; sondern zum Leben' [Not to Death But to Life], *Die Christengemeinschaft* 11/2019.
3. See Ravetz, Tom, *The Act of Consecration of Man.*
4. See Lauten, Johannes (ed.), *Die Schöpfung wartet auf den Menschen* [Creation Waits for Man], Urachhaus, Germany 2022.

5. Consultation: Remembrance and Renewal

1. Bonhoeffer, Dietrich *Akt und Sein, Transzendentalphilosophie und Ontologie in der systematischen Theologie* [Act and Being: Transcendental Philosophy and Ontology in Systematic Theology], Christian Kaiser Verlag, Germany 1988 p. 112.
2. Selg, Peter, 'Zwischen Ostern und Pfingsten – das Fünfte Evangelium heute' [Between Easter and Pentecost: The Fifth Gospel Today] in *Anthroposophie weltweit* [Anthroposophy Worldwide], Easter 2009.
3. Jung, C. G., *Symbols of Transformation, The Collected Works of C. G. Jung Volume 5,* Princeton University Press, USA 1968, paragraph 224.

4. Schad, Wolfgang, *Zeitbindung in Natur, Kultur und Geist* [Time Integration in Naure, Culture and Spirit], Verlag Freies Geistesleben, Germany 2016.

5. Meier, Ulrich, *Die Beichte. Atem der Liebe – das Sakrament der Menschwerdung* [Confession: Breath of Love – the Sacrament of the Incarnation].

6. Marriage: An Enhancement of Life's Potential

1. Steiner, Rudolf, *Vorträge und Kurse über christlich-religiöses Wirken* [Lectures and Courses on Christian Religious Work] (GA 343).
   See lecture of October 2, 1921.

2. Hüther, Gerald, *Etwas mehr Hirn* [A Little More Brain], Vandenhoeck & Ruprecht, Germany 2018.

3. See Gödecke, Susanne, *Die Trauung. Lebensweg zu zweit – ein frommer Wunsch?* [The Wedding: Life for Two – A Pious Wish?], Germany 2019.

4. Words cited from the second sentence of The Christian Community's creed.

7. Ordination: A Priestly Siblinghood

1. Jung, C.G., *Memories, Dreams, Reflections*, Fontana Press, UK 1995, p. 357.

2. See Bihin, Françoise, *Die Priesterweihe, Das Sakrament der Zukunft* [Ordination: The Sacrament of the Future], Urachhaus, Germany 2022.

3. Steiner, Rudolf *Vorträge und Kurse über christlich-religiöses Wirken* [Lectures and Courses on Christian Religious Work], p. 404f.

Bibliography

Arendt, Hannah, *The Human Condition*, University of Chicago Press, USA 2018.

Ravetz, Tom, *The Act of Consecration of Man*, Floris Books, UK 2020.

Steiner, Rudolf, *Christianity as Mystical Fact* (CW8), SteinerBooks, USA 2006.

—, *Social and Antisocial Forces in the Human Being*, Mercury Press, USA 1982.

—, *The Sun Mystery and the Mystery of Death and Resurrection* (CW211), SteinerBooks, USA 2006.

—, *Vorträge und Kurse über christlich-religiöses Wirken* [Lectures and Courses on Christian Religious Work] (GA 343), Verlag Goetheanum, Germany 1993.

Floris Books

For news on all our **latest books**, and to receive **exclusive discounts**, **join** our mailing list at:

florisbooks.co.uk

Plus subscribers get a FREE book with every online order!

We will never pass your details to anyone else.

Printed in the USA
CPSIA information can be obtained
at www.ICGtesting.com
JSHW012025200524
63489JS00011B/464

9 781782 508960